FEATHERED FARM ANIMALS

PHEASANTS

by Elizabeth Andrews

Cody Koala
An Imprint of Pop!
popbooksonline.com

Hello! My name is Cody Koala

This book is filled with videos, puzzles, games, and more! Scan the QR codes* while you read, or visit the website below to make this book pop.

popbooksonline.com/pheasant

*Scanning QR codes requires a web-enabled smart device with a QR code reader app and a camera.

abdobooks.com

Published by Pop!, a division of ABDO, PO Box 398166, Minneapolis, Minnesota 55439.

Printed in the United States of America, North Mankato, Minnesota.

082025
012026

Cover Photo: Shutterstock Images
Interior Photos: Adobe Stock; Shutterstock Images; Getty Images
Editors: Tyler Gieseke and Grace Hansen
Series Designer: Julia Line

Library of Congress Control Number: 2025940517

Publisher's Cataloging-in-Publication Data
Names: Andrews, Elizabeth, author.
Title: Pheasants / by Elizabeth Andrews
Description: Minneapolis, Minnesota : Pop!, 2026 | Series: Feathered farm animals | Includes online resources and index
Identifiers: ISBN 9781098248567 (lib. bdg.) | ISBN 9781098249083 (ebook)
Subjects: LCSH: Pheasants--Juvenile literature. | Poultry--Juvenile literature. | Fowls--Juvenile literature. | Farm animals--Juvenile literature. | Animal husbandry--Juvenile literature.
Classification: DDC 636.594--dc23

Table of Contents

Chapter 1

Meet the Pheasant!

Pheasants are birds. They live in groups called flocks. Female pheasants are called hens. Male pheasants are called cocks. They **cluck** and **crow**.

Watch a video here!

tail

Ring-necked pheasants are the most common on farms. Cocks are more colorful than hens. They have blue-green heads, white necks, red wattles, and long, bright tails. Hens have brownish feathers.

wattle
beak
wing
claw

Pheasants grow to be between 23 and 36 inches (58–91 cm) long. They

usually weigh 2 to 3 pounds (0.9–1.4 kg). They can fly short distances.

Chapter 2

Life on the Farm

Some farmers raise pheasants for their meat and eggs. Others raise pheasants to hunt. Pheasants raised for hunting live on **game farms**. Hunters visit these farms for enjoyment.

Learn more here!

Pheasants prefer to live outside. Many live in large pens that have lots of space to **roam** around. They need thick plants to hide and nest in. If there is not enough of this cover, pheasants fight.

Pheasant pens need to be covered with netting so the birds don't fly away.

Pheasants on game farms aren't kept in pens. Instead, they walk the land freely. Pheasants will choose **crop** fields, woods, and **wetlands** to live in.

Most hens only lay eggs in the spring. They nest on the ground. Healthy farm hens

Pheasant eggs are half the size of chicken eggs.

can lay up to 60 eggs a year. Pheasant eggs are green and brown in color.

Chapter 3

What Do They Eat?

Pheasants in pens often get special **feed**. It is a mix of animal and plant matter. Other pheasants eat plants, insects, worms, and seeds. All pheasants need fresh water.

Explore links here!

Chapter 4

Soft with Spots

Pheasant babies are called chicks. They **hatch** from eggs. They are light brown with spots. Chicks live indoors for the beginning of their lives to stay safe. They move outside at eight weeks old.

Chicks stay with their mom for 10 to 12 weeks.

Complete an activity here!

Making Connections

Text-to-Self

What is one new thing you learned about pheasants in this book?

Text-to-Text

Have you read any other books about farm animals? How were those animals similar to or different from pheasants?

Text-to-World

There are many kinds of pheasants. With the help of an adult, look up a few different types of pheasant. How are they similar to and different from the ring-necked pheasant?

Glossary

cluck – to make the sound of a hen.

crop – any plant that farmers grow.

crow – to make the loud sound of a cock.

feed – food designed for a specific kind of animal.

game farm – a place where animals are raised to be released into wildlife areas for hunting.

hatch – to break out of an egg.

roam – to move freely without purpose or direction.

wetland – land that is often covered by shallow water.

Index

Online Resources

popbooksonline.com

Thanks for reading this Cody Koala book!

This book is filled with videos, puzzles, games, and more! Scan the QR codes* while you read, or visit the website below to make this book pop.

popbooksonline.com/pheasant

*Scanning QR codes requires a web-enabled smart device with a QR code reader app and a camera.